COMING OUT OF THE BOX

My Journey to Purity and Identity

Shaniece F. Wauchope

DAYELight
PUBLISHERS

DAYELight
PUBLISHERS

Book Cover Design by HCP Book Publishing

ISBN: 978-1-949343-46-5

Table of Contents

Acknowledgement

$\mathcal{I}$ take this opportunity to express deep gratitude to everyone who has influenced my life in any way. God has used your contributions, even the negative ones, to shape the story of my life. I could not have been where I am today if our paths had not crossed, so thank you.

A special thank you to my family, especially my sister, Amoy, for your constant encouragement and invaluable support throughout the writing of this book.

Thank you to my pastor, Overseer D.A. Stennett, for the foundation of truth you gave that helped me to forgive my father.

Thank you to all my sisters in Christ for the role you played during the season that God was calling me out of the box and into my purpose. To all my friends who kept me in your prayers daily as I wrote this book, thank you. Your prayers paved the way for this release.

Thank you to my coach and sister, Crystal Daye, for helping me clarify the message that God gave me and for your support throughout this book-writing period. I know I frustrated you and even hid from you for a few months, but you remained patient with me and I am grateful.

Finally, I want to thank you, my readers, for the time you are going to invest in this book, and I pray that it will transform your lives and relationships with God.

DEDICATION

I choose to dedicate this book to a young lady who confided in me about her struggles with sexual sins. I could see your passion for God and the potential and impact that you were called to have in the kingdom of God. I could also see your fear, condemnation and refusal to do anything beyond attending church. Much like myself, I saw you wasting away under guilt and condemnation. I saw myself in your eyes. You remained my inspiration through the time I was fighting to be free and writing this book. You were much braver than me when you opened up that day and I knew then that I owed it to myself, and to you, to release this book. It is only fitting that this book be dedicated to you, the vessel God used to help me fight this subtle, yet crippling sin. I pray that this book will do for you what you did for me that day. Go forth and be free.

INTRODUCTION

———————————

*T*he memory of the inexplicable pleasure that rushed through me while lying on a bed with my friend on top of me was fresh in my mind. I had never felt pleasure like that in my few years on the earth. I was only eight years old. Even though I was embarrassed at first about what happened, I could not shake the desire of wanting to experience it again.

From the outside looking in, I had a life that anyone would desire, but on the inside things were on the rocks. My family was slowly falling apart. My young mind could not process the hurt I felt as the people I loved slowly walked out of my life. What was the point of living? Nobody loved me or seemed to care how I was being impacted by their actions. Rejected is the best word to capture the way I felt.

Consumed with my feelings of rejection, along with my desire to experience sexual pleasure, I embarked on a mission to belong and fulfill that desire. I longed for love, especially the love of a father. Men flocked me, and I gave in, since they were men, maybe I could find the love there. After all, I seemed to be important to them. Boy was I wrong! My life spiraled downwards until the day I could not hide from God anymore. After years of chasing me, I finally surrendered to the only One who could offer the love I needed, God.

My troubles did not end there. Life as a Christian has been challenging in many ways. I struggled to let go of the sexual fulfilment that lingered, and while I did not engage in sexual intercourse, masturbation was my way of release. I tried to convince myself that I was walking in purity and I did not have a problem. However, the conviction of the Lord proved otherwise. After years of indulging in this lifestyle, I finally found the courage and grace to break free. It was not an easy process but, thanks be to God, His grace is sufficient.

As if that was not enough, because of my desire to belong, I successful and perfectly lost the essence of who I was. After years of being in the church, I assimilated into the "box" of people's expectation, forgetting who God had called me to be.

"Coming Out Of The Box" will take you on a journey with me through many of the silly mistakes I made and how God rescued me in the nick of time. In this book, you will find out more about the circumstances that led me into promiscuity and how the Lord used my mess to save me.

Parents, I share how I indulged in many activities without the knowledge of my guardians. I was especially successful in concealing my actions because I maintained a good performance in school. I even went as far as sharing how I was influenced by the music I listened to and the movies I watched. I pray this book will show you the important task God has given you to shield your children from the enemy's devices.

"Coming Out Of The Box" will take you further into my journey as a Christian and my struggle to walk in sexual purity. I believed that the lack of sexual intercourse meant I was walking in purity, but that belief was faulty. I was bound to the sin of masturbation yet serving in church. Many of us look good and happy in church but are dying slowly from the sins that are keeping us bound.

My encounter with a youth who allowed me to see my life through her own life led me to fight to break free from this sin. The journey to freedom was rocky and scary as I encountered fierce demons in spiritual warfare. The process I went through led me to come up with a formula on how to break free from any sin and stay free.

Finally, this book brings to light my identity challenges and how it led me to losing myself in the church. I share how I knew that I was a child of God, restored by the blood of Jesus, yet lost the essence of what made me Shaniece, the individual.

People's expectations can box us in and lead to frustration and dissatisfaction. Walking in purpose becomes a fight when you are stuck in this box. As I commit to come out of the box, I also challenge you, my reader, to break free from whatever box you have placed yourself in. It is important to remember that God made us unique to fulfill unique purposes. This means that you must retain this uniqueness in the body of Christ to accomplish this purpose.

I pray the words written in the pages of this book will enlighten, encourage, and inspire you to break free from any sin you are struggling with, and equip you to walk in your God-given purpose.

Chapter 1
WHERE IT ALL STARTED

I grew up in a one-bedroom house with a kitchen, bathroom and living room, deep in the rural parish of St. Elizabeth, Jamaica. I was blessed to have both parents along with my older brother and sister living with me. For the first few years of my life things seemed perfect. I spent a lot of time with my mother and siblings as my mother was a stay-at-home mom. She sold grocery to help make life more comfortable. My father was not at home much as he owned several farms, so he went out early in the mornings and got back late in the nights. As much as I grew up in the country, I hated to go on the farm. I hated walking through the bushes to get there and I was terribly afraid of heights. Unfortunately for me, we had to go down some precipice at times. I greatly enjoyed every chance I got to spend with my father. I thought I was his favourite child. He even got upset with teachers who punished me at school as he never punished me when I was growing up.

Even more fun was when we got to visit our family in the neighbouring community. We spent time with our aunts and played with our cousins. There were other children the same age as my older siblings who joked around and called me aunt. Now imagine this light skin, short, chubby little child being called aunt by children twice her size. I did not like it one bit, but I still loved them.

As I grew older, I learned that my father had other children before he met my mom and that explained why I had nieces and nephews my age and older. I also realised that the reason my father came home so late was because he stopped at the bar to drink with friends. In his drunken state, he always called for his little daughter nicknamed "Mello." My mother and siblings gladly pushed me into the living room to have a singing party with him whenever he got home. When I was younger, those were the moments I cherished but as I got older, I became embarrassed.

Gradually, I started to realise that my perfect little world was not as perfect as I thought. My father's behaviour was very disturbing and when he got home late in the nights, he woke all of us. In an attempt to shield and protect us, my mom always tried to keep him out of the bedroom and that would lead to arguments. What was happening to my perfect home and family? I started to notice how unhappy my mother was. Most of the provisions that we needed were made by her. My father only took care of the food and bills; anything else we needed had to be provided by my mother. That is when I realised why she sold meat at home and often went to the market to sell produce and whatever else she could do to help us. I was often embarrassed, but she would also seek help from family members to find clothing for us to wear so it was very rare that we wore new clothing. Thank God for the good people we had in our lives who always extended a helping hand. Many people did not know what we were going through because family matters stayed at home. We barely had friends over, and we were rarely allowed to visit a friend's house. Naturally, you can imagine that sleeping over was a no-no, not even at my best friend's house.

In time my mother got a housekeeping job that allowed her to go into Kingston to work so she could provide better for us. Being the youngest, I often went with her during the summertime and spend my summer holidays there. I looked forward to that opportunity every time. While I loved school, I also loved holidays just as much because I could go to the city to spend time with different aunts.

I was not related to the family my mom worked with but, out of respect, I was told to call them aunt and uncle. They had a daughter close to my age. She was an only child and her parents were well-off financially, so she had everything to her comfort. I was happy about this because it meant more toys to play with when I went there. Luckily for me, this only child also did not mind sharing her toys. Only rarely we had a "fight" over something.

Visiting them was one of my favourite things to do. I remember passing out one day while playing on the swing her dad built in the mango tree. Did I mention how afraid I was of heights? Well, that day he pushed us so high in the air, all I remember was going closer and closer to the light peeping through the leaves of the mango tree. Then everything went black as I passed out.

While some of my greatest memories were created with this family, one of the worst memories was also created with them. I remember one summer when I went with my mom to visit them, they had changed homes. This new home was in a gated community with a smaller yard space and no more swing in the backyard. However, my friend had a new favourite hobby and that was roller skating. One day she tried to teach me, but I was not catching on very well. We soon got tired and decided to go upstairs to her bedroom to find something else to do. Something very unexpected happened in her room that day. I honestly do not remember the details of what happened but the next thing I knew I was lying on the bed on my back and my friend was on top of me moving her body in a circular motion. I experienced a pleasurable sensation that was very new to me. I was embarrassed so I did not tell anyone about it. I was so glad when my mom stopped working there so I would not have to spend time with her anymore.

I tried my best to forget about that day and what had happened in that bedroom, but there was something about what I felt that made me curious to find out more. I was scared to tell anyone about it or ask questions because of the fear of what might happen or what they would say. I was about eight years old and things relating to sex were not as exposed as it is now.

That feeling would not leave my mind. I needed to figure out how to relive that experience. In my curiosity I started to experiment with myself until I was finally able to relive that moment of pleasure. It was at that tender age that I began a life of masturbation without understanding what I was doing. Now that I am much older, I realise that many persons discovered this phenomenon in different ways, and it was not an uncommon thing. However, I believe that without this incident, it was very unlikely that I would have discovered it.

Amidst all of this, things were only getting worse at home. There was no ignoring the obvious unhappiness my mother endured to keep us secure. I remember wanting her out of the situation so badly. Enough was enough. I started to resent my father. Sometimes I wished that he would not come home because when he did the place became so heavy and unhappy.

Somewhere along the line, my mother gave her life to Christ and we started to spend a lot of time at church. Sunday mornings and evenings, we were there and always early. We never missed a Bible study service or youth meetings. My mother's commitment to God inspired me to give my life to Christ at the tender age of eight years old. She not only went to church, but she prayed long and hard for our family and the people in our community. Her passion and dedication to God was very inspiring to me as a child. However, I could not help but observe that the more dedicated she became, the more things gradually got worse in our home.

After a few years, it was almost as if my mother lost her will to fight. She was done, and she needed to leave. I understood, to a small extent, what was happening. I was about ten years old at that point. I honestly just wanted her out of the situation. A part of me was glad and relieved for her when she left, but reality struck me when she did not take me with her. As children, we tend not to think too far in the future about the consequences that come with every decision. I did not think about the fact that my mother leaving meant that I would be left without the guidance of a mother. I surely did not think that the security and certain comfort would be stripped away.

When the reality of what happened finally hit me, I concluded that God had failed me and my family. I know many persons reading this would try to judge my mother, but you never know what you will do until you are in a similar situation. If this God loved me so much, why didn't He fix my family? Why didn't He help my mother when she needed Him the most? To top it all off, the church we were so dedicated to did not intervene. I remember one of the comments that was passed about the circumstances surrounding why my mother left; I was hurt. Who gave them the right to say anything bad about her? Where were they when she was going through what she went through? Why didn't they do something about it? I never saw the support being returned to her by the church.

I turned my back on God and the church. If my mother had been so dedicated and they failed her,

I was not about to waste my life serving God only to get the same results. I was young and lacked understanding. I did not know that what they did in the church did not reflect who God was, it was only the inadequacies of man and not God. But isn't that what happens when we are hurt by the church? We bypass man, the church and jump right to blaming God. I blamed God for many years.

So, after my mother left, it was only me, my father, brother and sister. Sometime after, my brother also left to live with my aunt. It was now up to my father to raise me and my sister. In all honesty, I can see where he tried. He was sober more often, he tried not to stay out as late as he used to, and he cooked at times to ensure that we were not hungry. But it takes more than that to take care of girls, especially on the brink of puberty. I guess, given the circumstances, he did the best he could.

I hated him for years as he was responsible for the destruction of my beautiful world but today, I am grateful for him. As I reflect, I realise he could have neglected us after my mom left but he tried his best. You see, a lot of times we try to belittle our parents based on the little that they did for us growing up but never pause to think that they were trying to give us more than they received from their parents. I learned this truth from my Pastor. I believe with each generation parents resolve in their hearts that there are certain things their children will never go through or never lack. Let us bear this in mind and if you have something against your parents, you need to work through it. The Holy Spirit will help you, if you ask Him.

Even though I knew that my mother's leaving had nothing to do with me and she could not take me with her, I could not help but question my value. I could not help feeling rejected. To add to this, my father and sister did not get along so there was always a quarrel in the house. My sister was only fourteen years old. Imagine being required to take care of a home, a younger sister and yourself at that age. She became overwhelmed and, eventually, she went to live with a friend who lived closer to her school. I had to learn to take care of myself. Thank God for neighbours who tried to lend support where they could. In spite of their efforts, I felt like I was all alone in the world, like I had no one and nobody cared about me. Rejection was at its peak in my life. I became bitter and angry at the world.

As is customary when a girl starts to get older, boys start to notice her, even men. Sure enough, I started getting attention from men and I stopped feeling so insignificant. Even though I knew what they wanted, I was grateful for the attention. I eventually stopped going to church. So, with no mother around, and no church to keep me in check, I could do just about anything I wanted to. Thankfully, the principles I learned in church while growing up still grounded me to an extent. If I did not have that spiritual grounding, I would have been very promiscuous. Therefore, the Bible says: "Train up a child in the way he should go, and when he is old, he will not depart from it" (Proverbs 22:6). When God has a purpose for your life, He will find ways to sow seeds of His word into your heart even from a tender age. But I guarantee the enemy will also sow his own negative seeds in hope of corrupting God's plan.

Chapter 2
Curiosity Peaked

When I started high school, I was determined to defy every moral standard that I got at church. I was done with God and things concerning Him. I started to do everything I was told not to do. I grew up in a Pentecostal church that was against the wearing of makeup, jewelry, pants, extensions and the processing of hair. The first thing I did was process my hair, then I started to wear pants. Everything was starting to change. Finding out more about boys was my priority. I was so shielded that at one point I thought it was a sin to like a guy. So, maybe I was too young but, at the end of the day, I still had questions that I was not comfortable asking. I wanted to fully explore the desires I had.

After my first term, I was engaging in conversations with different guys until I started to date a guy who was several grades ahead of me. I thought I was accomplished, and I behaved as though I was. I was not engaged in sexual activities yet, but I loved the thrill of just being able to say I was dating an older guy and he "loved" me. One day, while going about my day at school, I was confronted by another girl my age.

"Yuh an Tony deh?" (Are you dating Tony?) She asked.

"Yeh, a wah?" (Yes, why?) was my response.

To my surprise, she told me that she was also dating Tony. I was distraught! Instead of us fighting each other, we decided to confront him. The story ended with him dumping both of us. I was dumped for the first time and I determined in my heart that it would be the first and last. Based on my background, I had a low perception of men and this only made it worse. I did not know I could have become any more bitter than I already was, but I did.

After the incident, I had only one intention and that was to hurt every male I came in contact with. I became friends with mostly boys. I needed to learn more about them, to understand what they look for in girls. Once I learned this, I became that kind of girl. I was on a life's mission to destroy every man. I had little self-value, but I had a mission bigger than me. I was a bit saddened that the young man who helped to compound the low perception I had of men did not get the chance to pay. There is a local saying in Jamaica, "If yuh cyaah ketch Quaco, yuh ketch him shut" meaning if you cannot hurt your offender, hurt someone close to them. That is exactly what I set out to do. Looking back now, it was very silly because the only person I ended up hurting was ultimately myself. Although I desperately wanted to hurt men, I had an even greater desire to experience a love from them that only a father could give.

I remember after school my girlfriends and I hung out with boys who were way too old. To put things into perspective, I was about thirteen years old. That was fifteen years ago; can you imagine what our children are up to now? Especially given the fact that they are more exposed to sexual contents. We were flirting with guys, kissing and messing around until late in the evenings. Not that I was accountable to anyone, but it was easy to explain because we did all that at the library. So, I could have easily said I went to the library. But, of course, it did not matter because I knew when I got home no one would be there. Besides, mom was too far to even do anything.

After messing around with boys who I had no interest in, I was finally afforded the opportunity to do what I ultimately wanted to do; have sex. I met a guy and though we were not in a relationship, he seemed to be the perfect candidate to give me the experience I longed for. He was not the most attractive person but still the ideal candidate because of convenience. Only after I found my identity in Christ did I become heartbroken by my foolish actions. I did not know anything about the value of my virginity, all I knew was that I had this desire that I was bent on fulfilling no matter what.

I am heartbroken by this fact now because the one thing I really desire to give to my husband, I do not have it to give. I implore you, my dear sister, hold on to this gift that God has given you until the day you meet the man with whom you desire to spend the rest of your life. If, like me, you have already made the mistake, God is able to restore.

Parents, start teaching your children the value of remaining pure. Do not just state it as a rule not to be debated but help them to understand why it is important.

My mission continued. I remember after making several attempts to have sex with the guy, I finally decided that it was not going to work for now. It was more painful than I anticipated. I reverted to flirting and kissing. Amidst this, I remained focused on my schoolwork. I was not foolish; I knew education was my ticket to a better life.

As if by some motherly intuition, my mother swooped in to rescue me. She found a lovely lady who was happy to take me into her home under her care. At first, I was excited about it because it meant I would have some structure to my life, and I was finally going to receive some semblance of love. However, deep down I was not truly happy because what I really wanted was to be with my mother.

If you thought the rebellion in me died when this lady took me in, you surely thought wrong. It got worse. She was a beautiful soul and she tried her best, but at that time it did not mean much to me. I do not believe she was equipped to deal with someone who had endured so much rejection and brokenness. On the surface, you would never imagine the way I was feeling. I had become an expert at being the right person for the situation I was in. I wore masks for everyone to the point where I began to lose my true self. I had no sincere regard for anyone around me as it was all about self-preservation.

Things really started to go downhill when she attempted to exert authority and tried to discipline me. It is not that I did not respect her, but I had become so accustomed to doing my own thing. I did not know how to handle authority. I really hoped it would have been a new beginning for me, but my rejection did not stop there. On one occasion it was made very clear to me by one of her family members that I did not belong in her family or in her home. Wow! This compounded the belief in my mind that I belonged nowhere. Instead of me getting better, I only got worse.

Notwithstanding, I still had a mission to accomplish. Now that I was in a new environment where no one knew me, it was the ideal place for me to unleash. I realised that I could do whatever I pleased without being judged by anyone because no one knew that I had been in church and they had no way of finding out. Most students attending my new school was from the inner city. Their exposure to violence and sex was beyond my scope. While such an environment would have intimidated others, it was ideal to help me accomplish my goal.

Fortunate for me, my skin bore no scars, it is almost flawless. This attracted men from all walks of life. I became so self-centered and self-focused, it was all about me, myself and I. It did not take long for me to become popular among both students and teachers. I was one of the top performers in my entire grade and I was very personable, so I got along with most of the students. Guys were not shy to make passes at me, but I was very picky about the boys that I was interested in. I wanted the tall, dark and handsome ones. I was not very interested in committed relationships and my mission to get back at men was still in high gear. I got close to one of my classmates. He became my good friend, but I was never interested in a relationship with him. He was instrumental in improving my understanding of the male species.

I had my eyes on one guy who I found to be very attractive. I made it clear to that young man that I desired him (sigh, it is sad the way I was) but he would not entertain me. He did, however, introduce me to a friend of his. He was not ideally who I wanted but I still had a mission that I needed to accomplish, so I settled for him.

The relationship started and moved pretty fast. I decided that it was time to brave up and experience what sex was like. We planned it out and executed our plan. One day after school when everything was set, my two friends and I went to a house in a community I was not familiar with. Each of us had our partners and the mission was accomplished. It was not easy as the pain was excruciating but it was now or never. I braved up and went all the way.

Sadly, shortly after, I discovered that this boyfriend of mine was dating several other girls. I thought we had something going but, unfortunately, he was playing a numbers game and because of my own desperation to lose my virginity I fell into that number. I was hurt for a while and purposed in my heart not to get involved with anyone else. But that only lasted a couple months.

I decided to walk away from schoolboys because they were just not mature enough for me. I should have been walking away from relationships and focusing solely on school but that was the farthest thing from my mind. Nevertheless, I thank the Lord every day for my Spanish teacher. She was the only voice at the time reiterating the Word of God to me. She spent a portion of her class talking about God and the importance of valuing ourselves. Many did not listen to her and I pretended that I didn't either but deep down she was making an impact. I remember her sharing a story of how her husband waited until their wedding day to kiss her for the first time because he valued her and if a man was not willing to wait for us, then he did not truly love us.

I did not want to receive what she was sharing at the time because I thought she was a crazy lady who wanted to stop us from being ourselves and enjoying life. I came this far; I was not about to let her stop me. I had the same mentality I can now identify in a lot of youths today, "me against the world." At that point in my life, I could not see that she was coming from a place of love and compassion. I just knew that I wanted to live life my own way and she was not going to get in the way of that. As a matter of fact, no one was going to get in the way.

CHAPTER 3
MY ADDICTIONS

$\mathcal{N}$ow that the uncertainty of what sex entailed was gone, I was ready to launch out and have new experiences. Men no longer had to pursue me, if I wanted you, I would let you know and then I would have you. So many things transpired in my life as a high school student that no one to this day believes me when I tell them the type of person I was before finding my identity in Christ.

When I just started high school, I remember there was a man in my childhood community who always told me about sex. He made it sound appealing, but I always told him that I was not interested in that yet, even though I internalised what he said. I distinctly remember him telling me that once I started, I would enjoy it so much that I would not want to stop. I never forgot his words, and I realised they were true. Let me pause again to beseech all parents reading this book, do not be afraid to have the sex talk with your children because people are out there waiting eagerly to teach them the wrong things about sex.

Even though I was not interested in dating schoolboys anymore, I still had fun with them but never sex, they did not qualify for that anymore. I needed someone more mature, I needed a man, so I set out on a search. I did not have to search long or hard because one day my friend decided she was going to a guy's house. I am not even sure if they were dating but he was not in school. She invited me to go with her and, of course, I followed her because that was how we rolled. I wondered what I would do because no one wanted to be the third wheel in those situations. When I got there, someone was already lined up to keep my company while she handled her business. I was about fifteen years old.

I was not in the mood for this man because even though I said I wanted a big man; I did not mean this old. We were sitting in a room and talking but there was no denying that the chemistry between us was overwhelmingly strong. That day marked the beginning of our relationship; the relationship that I was looking for.

I went to his house almost every day after school. I cannot quite remember how I pulled it off because I was not living on my own. I think I probably told my guardian that I had extra classes or something. This man's house was my safe haven. He treated me right, I felt like I mattered to him. I found the love and worth that I was looking for all those years; the love like that of a father. What I liked most was that he insisted that I put school first. If, for some reason, I started to fall back in school, he would distance himself because he thought he was the distraction. I remember he would ask me about my days and dreams, and he encouraged me a lot. There were days when I just laid beside him or with my head on his chest and he would hold me in his arms and tell me how beautiful I was and how much I meant to him and I believed every word he said. I felt so secured in his arms. "I could do this for a lifetime," I thought.

Unfortunately, it did not last long. One day, an incident took place that changed our relationship. This once loving man simply dismissed me from his life. I did not hear from him anymore. He stopped answering my calls and I could not just show up at his house unannounced. I was crushed. Just when I thought there was hope for me finding love, worth and security, he left me hanging. Men were failing me too badly. I did not realise at the time that I was trying to find love and worth in all the wrong places. What was the point? I tried to block everything about that relationship from my mind; I simply could not handle those memories. I struggled to forgive him for what he did to me. When I got older, he tried to make up for the wrong he did, but that chapter of my life was long closed.

I concluded that it was not just schoolboys who had a problem, but it was men on a whole, so I was done seeking serious relationships. Or that was what I was hoping to achieve, even though it did not quite work out that way. It was clear that relationships were not my thing, yet I continued with them just the same.

In addition to my strong desire to belong to someone, my addiction to sex was very real, and I could not seem to break away from it. As loose as I was, I never really believed that I was low enough to sleep with any and every random guy and so I needed to be in a "relationship" no matter how short-lived it was. In my mind, doing that would keep me from being promiscuous. So that is what my relationships became about, sex. I also became focused on hurting men the way they had been hurting me. I would learn exactly what they were looking for and be the perfect girl, setting them up even to the point of having sex and then walked away. I look back at my life and realise that it was only the grace of God why I did not die brutally. I took many dangerous risks, hurting myself in the process without even realising or even caring. I thought I had nothing to live for. I ended up in many toxic relationships, but GOD!

CHAPTER 4
LUSTFUL DESIRES

I was slowly but surely spiraling downwards. Whatever my mind conceived, I would set out to achieve.

After years of being separated from my mother, I finally got the opportunity to live with her again. Initially, I was ecstatic about it because it was what I always wanted. However, my excitement was short-lived because I had to abide by her rules, which was not ideal for me. She was not the humble Christian mother I had growing up. Living with my mom, of course, did not stop my notorious lifestyle. I just had to be more cautious because mothers have a way of sensing when things are not right.

Eventually, I had to move away from my mom again because of the distance between where she lived and the school I was attending. That is when my aunt stepped in and offered me a place in her home. I was grateful, but things became tense between me and my aunt as we did not see eye to eye on most things.

I needed to de-stress and the only way I knew how was to find a new boy-toy. This new boyfriend was tall, dark and handsome but we could not get along. Our constant arguing was putting a strain on the relationship. Sex was not proving to be a good enough reason to stick around. However, I still held on because it was better than being single.

Looking back, I can only smile, because in spite of all my mess and rebellion, God was still actively shielding me. I think one of the major things He shielded me from was getting pregnant. I remember right before my final exams, my period was late, and I was losing my mind. I needed to study but I could not focus. To top it off, my boyfriend did not take it seriously. I was scared. We did not get along so if I had a child with him, I would be stuck interacting with him for the rest of my child's life. Besides, I was too young to have a child. I had my whole life ahead of me. I remember praying, "Lord, please don't let me be pregnant." I had physics exam the following day and I needed to study but I kept going to the bathroom checking and praying to see one red spot. No such luck. I somehow managed to pass the exam, thanks be to God.

When I found out I was not pregnant, I quickly ended the relationship. I decided to lay low for a while; no more relationships, no more sex. However, I was still hooked on masturbation and pornography.

Chapter 5
Surrendered Or Not

One day, while hanging out with my friend after school, I saw a young man that I knew would be my next boyfriend. He was not the usual dark-skinned guy that I dated, and I did not even like the school he attended, but I liked him. Even though I had vowed to stay away from schoolboys, there was something different about him. He was a Christian. Not a very solid one, but the Lord used him in the grand scheme of things to draw me back to Him.

Most of our conversations were about God and church. I even visited churches to impress him. With each visit to church, the conviction of God became stronger and I knew the Lord was calling me back to a relationship with Him. However, I would never surrender because I thought I would lose my boyfriend and he was the only reason I was going to church. I had a fear for God that made me afraid of having sex with him because he was a Christian.

Although things were going well in the relationship, I still had my underlying trust issues. I believed that he was cheating on me and my insecurity led me to cheat on him. When he found out, I thought it would have been the end of our relationship but, surprisingly, he was willing to forgive and make it work. That could have been a lifetime relationship, but his level of commitment scared me. I ended the relationship without a valid reason. There are some decisions we live to regret; I cannot help but think what could have been if I was not so immature. Nevertheless, I believe that relationship served its purpose in getting God back on the radar in my life.

Shortly after meeting that young man, I started a new school which had a better Christian grounding. In that environment, there was no escaping God. However, I refused to surrender as I could not give up this "wonderful" life of "freedom" that I had. The new friends I made were mostly Christians, and they were not shy about sharing their faith with me. I even found it annoying. They were always inviting me to some prayer meeting or other meetings their Christian group was having.

In 2010, during my second year of attending the new school, my sister accepted Christ into her life. I should have been happy for her, but I could not help being upset. Although I was not living with her and my mother, each time I visited we would go partying together. My mother only allowed me to go out if my sister was there. Can you imagine how enraged I was when I found out that all that would change? I considered my sister to be selfish as she did not think about how her decision would affect me and the fun times we could have together. It never crossed my mind that I was being the selfish one.

Nevertheless, I decided that I would not let her decision affect me. She was not going to stop me from enjoying my life. So, on my next visit to my mom, I cleared out all her party clothes with the intention of wearing them. Shortly after, my mom excitedly shared the news of her own salvation with me. Slowly, my life was starting to fall apart. The thing is, I grew up in church, so I knew what it meant to be in relationship with God. I was partly happy for both her and my sister but deep down I was jealous.

Their salvation started to amplify the call of God in my ears. I was running out of places to hide. My ability to ignore His voice was growing weaker. However, I was still stubborn and set in my ways. I was not ready to give up my lifestyle.

After being single for a while, I decided that I was single for too long and I needed to find someone new. The new school was very different from what I was used to, so in addition to the fact that I did not see many prospects, I was not comfortable approaching anyone. I went through almost an entire term without a relationship, until my eyes caught someone of interest. He was distractingly hot. I was so distracted that school year that I performed poorly. My conversations with God receded to, "Lord, please let him talk to me."

I gladly embraced the summer holiday as school was becoming a struggle. One day, while browsing the internet, a message came in on my Facebook page. I did not know the person and even after he identified himself, I still could not believe who it was. Could it be? Was this really happening? Did God answer my prayers so soon? All those questions rushed into my mind at once. Yes, you guessed correctly! My crush was finally talking to me. I was shocked and elated. God did answer my prayer; or so I thought.

That relationship would have been wrong for me on many different levels but that made it even more intriguing. I was looking forward to a new adventure. I had concluded that committed relationships were not for me, thus, even the knowledge of his girlfriend did not dissuade me. I was not planning on allowing anything to stop me from living my life to the fullest. Not to mention that I was being empowered by the various movies and music that I was watching and listening to. Let me pause again to implore parents, be careful of what you allow your children to watch and listen to. They may seem harmless, but you do not know the hidden desires in your children that they are feeding. You have a responsibility to guard them.

As you have gathered by now, I moved around a lot. Shortly after that relationship started, I moved to live with my cousin. She was hardly home, so most of the time I had the house all to myself. I could literally do anything I wanted to, and that was exactly what I did. I quickly got busy making arrangements for my boyfriend to have sleepovers. I felt like I was living the best season of my life. My performance in school started to improve as I was no longer distracted with daydreaming about my crush.

My sister's baptismal service drew nearer, and she was sure to invite me. I was not prepared for what was about to take place. When I visited her church, I felt this warmth and love. It was like the people knew me and I was a part of their family. As I sat through the sermon, I had to question whether the pastor knew me. His sermon was pointed, and it felt as though I was the only person in the church, and he was addressing me directly.

Nevertheless, I would not yield to the Holy Spirit. But, as I watched my sister go under that water and got up, something melted in my heart. God spoke to me in that moment and I knew I could not run away from Him anymore. But, how could I possibly survive without sex? I simply could not. I continued to fight with everything that remained in me.

To my dismay, all the conversations with my mom, sister and friends seemed to be about God. I found every single excuse I could think of to explain why it was not the time for me. Some of the excuses were genuine but others were not. I could not deny that the Lord was calling me. I would end up at the altar crying every time I attended a church service, but I refused to surrender. I was not ready to give up everything.

Finally, I could not fight my convictions anymore; it was time. I made a deal with God, "Lord, I know You are calling me, and my time is short. I will serve You but give me the chance to have sex with my boyfriend one last time and then I am ready. Is that okay with You, Lord? Great!" I set off to plan my final night because, in my head, God had agreed with this plan of mine.

I got myself ready and made sure everything was set because it was my last time before I had to give it all up until I got married, if I ever did. My boyfriend came over and we got right down to business. However, something happened that was not a part of the plan. In the midst of the fun, I felt the presence of the Lord enter the room that night. My night of pleasure became a night of horror and dishonour. I felt as though my father walked in and caught me in the act. I could feel His hurt and disappointment. For the first time, I came face to face with my sins. I felt dirty before Him. Without any warning, I burst into tears; I could not hold them back.

My boyfriend almost went crazy trying to figure out what he did to hurt me. I could not explain at that point because my heart was so sorrowful at the hurt I was causing my heavenly Father. "I can't do this anymore. You have to leave," I told my boyfriend. I had to get my life together. This was now more than me. That night, I cleaned myself up. I cleaned my room, changed my sheets, removed all lude pictures, videos and music from my phone. That night started my journey of surrender to God. There was no more running or hiding from Him.

Chapter 6
False Purity

I did not get baptised immediately, but I continued to visit a church close to me. I did not explain to my boyfriend what happened that night out of fear that he would think I was crazy. I was not quite ready to end the relationship, even though sex was no longer going to be a factor. I still desired companionship. When I finally got the courage, I explained to my boyfriend that I was going to surrender my life to God which means things could not continue the same way. At the time he seemed to understand.

I became more involved in the Christian club at school that most of my friends were in. I started to attend all their prayer meetings willingly and any other event they hosted. The passion those young people had for God really inspired me to seek God more. After being around them for some time, my own desire for the Lord and the things concerning Him were growing quickly.

Certain habits, for example, drinking, partying, the use expletives and listening to violent and sex-oriented music were shedding within a few months. I could see the hand of the Lord in my life even before I got baptised. However, I was struggling to let go of my relationship, thus, I convinced myself that I could make it work. I convinced myself that my boyfriend would see how important this journey was to me and eventually join me.

I excitedly invited my boyfriend to my baptism because I wanted him to share this special moment with me. Much to my dismay he did not turn up. Although he claimed to support my decision, he was not showing it. Not once did he visit church with me, yet I refused to let go of the relationship. Now that I reflect on it, he was the same person who I knew had a girlfriend when I went into the relationship with him. Therefore, the kind of commitment I was seeking from him was just not going to happen. Still, I held on to him. One of our encounters got so intense that we ended up kissing and would have gone further if the environment was conducive. I knew I had to end the relationship, so I did. I had to cut off all ties, conversations and interactions. That was the only way I was going to move on.

My life was finally coming together. I found a place of love and acceptance at my church. I had a good relationship with my mom and sister. I became a member of the choir, but the question remained, "How was I going to manage being single?" I was always in a relationship with someone. I honestly did not think it was possible, so I went searching. Unfortunately, no suitors were found in my church. The only ones that were attractive were either married, engaged, or dating.

What on earth did I get myself into? I could not see how I was going to handle this new life. Matter of fact, I did not intend to; I needed to be in a relationship. If I could not find a man in the church, then I would find one outside and bring him in. That is what I set out to do. So, I went on a search outside the church. I found many suitors out there, encouraged them to Christ under the pretense that I really wanted them to be saved, which I did, but my main motive was me finding a husband. Almost all of them wanted sex and I was not willing to give that. Eventually I gave up and decided to try things God's way, trusting that He would give me the strength. I thought I was fully surrendered.

I was single and trying my best to remain pure before God. I could not engage in sexual relationships and be looked upon as a hypocrite. Before becoming a Christian, I despised folks who claimed to be Christians, yet were living a double life. I had to keep my legs together. The only way I knew how to do that was to distance myself from men. It was not easy, but I tried with all my might. Persons even said I had a "holier than thou" attitude but they would not know the pressure I was under. I could not trust myself to be in any private location with any man; old, young, ugly, cute or indifferent. The risk was too great. Souls were at risk, not only mine, but the souls of those who were looking to Christians for the light.

Being single was harder than I anticipated but I was slowly getting the hang of it. When I thought that I had everything under control, I fell back into the old habit of masturbation. With all the focus being on staying away from men and relationships, I did not take time to consider that masturbation was also considered sexual immorality. All I knew was that no one else was involved and it was not affecting any other soul. I tried to convince myself that it was well with me but deep down I felt otherwise. I felt filthy before the Lord. If I were to be honest with myself, I would have admitted that I had an issue, but my mind started drifting back to all the "glory days" when I used to indulge in the act. It became harder for me to focus on the conviction I was feeling. I fell into it again and again. I knew I needed to overcome that sin, but I was not sure I was ready to.

CHAPTER 7
GOT GUILT

I know many persons take the sin of masturbation lightly and many think it is harmless, but no sin is harmless. I got to a place where I was trying to make it up to God for messing up in that way. I read many articles online where Christians said it was okay, even leaders. I tried to appease my mind with those words, but it never quite helped.

I was convicted to my core. I did everything possible to ensure that I did not indulge again. However, each time I thought I was over it, I fell again. The urges were so forceful that every sense of reasoning faded, and my only goal was to feed the desire. I continuously failed the Lord. I started to question whether I was truly saved. My relationship with God was under severe strain because I did not think He wanted anything to do with me. I felt like such a hypocrite. Those thoughts were driving me crazy. I could not pray. Why would God want to hear from me? In spite of that, I smiled with everyone, trying to keep up appearances.

It eventually got worse. The once infrequent act was becoming more frequent and I did not seem to have any control over it. Not to mention the thoughts that flooded my mind. I needed help. If you have ever struggled with this sin, you know the embarrassment that comes with it so, of course, my first instinct was not to share my struggle with anyone. Who could I share it with? Everyone seemed to have this Christian walk under control. Besides, I was not about to become the public discussion of the church. I felt like I could trust no one. Therefore, I concluded that I had to deal with it on my own.

As time went by, the feelings and thoughts grew more intense. I felt hopeless and alone. Despite the feelings of hopelessness and despair that plagued me, I never gave up. I had nowhere else to turn. If God could not help me, then I was doomed. There had to be hope for me.

To make matters worse, leaders in the church started asking me to take part in the services more. I declined but they insisted. Then I started to wonder if they were spiritually blind. How could they miss that I was struggling with this issue? Finally, I concluded that since they insisted, maybe it was God leading them to be so persistent.

The burden of the struggle became heavier with each passing day. I felt like such a hypocrite, smiling and carrying on as though it was well with my soul, but I was silently dying. I dragged through each day hoping and praying.

I read numerous articles online that were meant to help me overcome. The advices were plenteous. Some of them worked but only temporarily and others made matters worse. Everything seemed to be a trigger for me. I was more attracted to my own body than I was to any man. I sank deep into depression. "Maybe this was my fate," I often thought. I was losing the will to fight.

A sermon was preached one Sunday on the topic of masturbation. It was one of the most condemning messages I sat through. The preacher was clear that masturbation was a sin. He described it as an act of having sex with demons and partaking in rituals. I waited and waited and prayed for him to mention in that sermon how to stop doing it. Well, I am still waiting. I can imagine that others who were secretly struggling with this sin also sat waiting for the solution too. "Wow," I thought, "I was not only sinning but having sex with demons." I sank into a deeper level of depression after that. What was the point? I was trying to fight this thing for so long and each time I thought I overcame, I just lapsed right back into it.

A couple months after that, the preacher returned with the same sermon on the topic. This time he offered a little help by saying "Stop it!" Could it really be that easy? If it was, why was I still struggling? The only good thing he offered that day were the names of the demons that were said to be the drivers of the act.

CHAPTER 8
SPIRITUAL WARFARE

*I*t is never a good place to be as a Christian where you have lost your will to fight against any sin, no matter how small and insignificant it may seem. The enemy will devour you. I craved help. I prayed and asked God to send help without me having to open up and share with anyone about my struggle.

I felt like a sex slave to an evil man and whenever he came, he was so forceful I had to drop everything and give in. The word sex was a trigger. I did not have to watch porn; my own body was a trigger. My body became a prison and I was losing hope.

I remember always praying to the Lord for help. I prayed defeated prayers because that was how I felt. I never struggled with the major sins like adultery and fornication, but this seemingly insignificant sin was enough to destroy me. The guilt was slowly killing me. I knew God had called me to great things, but I was not qualified to do anything.

My mother started to listen to teachings about spiritual warfare. At first, I considered it to be inconvenient because it was always so loud when I was trying to focus on other things. Eventually, the teachings started to interest me, and I paid keener attention. Then I remembered the names of the demons the preacher at my church mentioned and I started to do some research on them: incubus and succubus. I was now understanding the reason behind my overwhelming desires.

I know masturbation is accepted as a natural practice that is fully endorsed by the medical fraternity as a way of releasing sexual frustration. However, you know you are being controlled by these spirits when your desires become so overwhelming that it interferes with your normal activities. I was on to the spirits and I found my will to fight again. I knew what I was up against and I was not going to be held hostage by those demons anymore.

I started watching more videos and reading articles to better equip myself. I knew the enemy was not happy. One night, as I was about to go to sleep, the Holy Spirit put me on my guard and told me not to be afraid. That night, while I was sleeping, I was lying on my left side with my face turned to the wall. A monstrous being came on my bed and it held my hands above my head and sank its claws into my feet. As fear started to grip me, I remembered the Lord's word that I should not be afraid. Immediately, I started to call the name of Jesus, but no sound was coming from my lips. Nevertheless, I would not give up. I kept repeating it in my head until it blurted from my mouth audibly. I felt empowered by the Holy Spirit and I pleaded the blood of Jesus against that monster until it let me go and fell off my bed. I looked over and saw it curled up at the side of my bed and I kept rebuking it until it disappeared. It was so real. I jumped out of my sleep searching my hands and feet for scars. Even as I write this, I can feel the claws sinking into my skin. I was traumatized! The thought came to my head that if I had not been poking around and messing with those demons, then I would not have had that experience. Out of fear, I stopped all my research because I did not want to have another encounter like that ever again.

I went back to praying my normal defeated prayers, begging God to help me when, clearly, He had empowered me to fight. However, fear had crippled me, and I did not want to engage that demon again. No thank you! That was exactly what the enemy wanted, and he crept right back into my life and started to overpower me again through fear.

CHAPTER 9
STRUGGLING WITH PERVERSION

I had settled back into life the way it was. I was still struggling but too afraid to do anything about it. I accepted it as my fate and, I guess, I decided I had to live with it. I never stopped praying but I was not willing to do whatever it took, if it meant entering into warfare against that demon or telling the struggle to someone.

The Lord drew my attention to a young lady at my church. I could see that the calling of God was great on her life; she was full of potential. Each time she was asked to do something in church that I knew she was capable of doing, she declined. I could not understand why she was not allowing herself to be used by God. I pried until one day she finally shared her struggle with the sin of masturbation and pornography. Immediately I saw myself through her; how I was wasting away in this life riddled with guilt and condemnation. I saw how much potential I had yet I would not allow God to use me the way He wanted to. It all became crystal clear. After speaking with her, I went home and made a vow to the Lord. "Lord, if you deliver me from this sin, I promise to help deliver your people." That, my friend, was the vow that led to the writing of this book. The fear of engaging in warfare paled against the determination to help that young lady. I knew the only way to help her would be to break free.

I resumed my research and started to spend more time seeking God on the matter. I tried to muster the courage to show a video at my church on the same topic, but I could not because I was not yet delivered. As you can imagine, the attacks intensified. However, the attacks did not manifest as nightmares but as an overwhelming desire to masturbate. I tried my best to fight but I felt out of control. Hopelessness started to consume me once more and the enemy began to overpower me through condemnation.

Nevertheless, the Lord was teaching me. I realised that there was more to it than meets the eye. The

70

Lord had me observe the seasons that the attacks would get intense. I noticed that it happened most when I was asked to do anything at church, when I had a great experience with God or a huge success in my relationship with Him. You see, I never realised that in the past because I was too busy feeling guilt-riddened. My understanding of spiritual dynamics was growing.

One of the prayers that I came across addressed generational curses. I was repeating that prayer for a while without even thinking it through. But the Lord drew me back to my own father and the lifestyle that he lived. He was promiscuous and perverted in many ways. Prior to that, I never thought much about the impact his actions had on me. However, I was learning that the spirits that influenced him were being passed on to his children. That explained many things. I do not know much about my siblings' private life, so I did not know if it had impacted them as much as it did me. However, I became resolute that I would break that curse from over my family. I was slowly being equipped with bits and pieces of information that were essential to my deliverance.

As I sat in a bus one day, on my way to school, my mind was flooded with thoughts that caused me to question my salvation. Suddenly, this thought came to me, "You are so perverted." I repeated to myself, "I am so perverted." As if a lightbulb turned on in my head, another thought came to me, "Why not pray against the spirit of perversion?" I immediately googled prayers against the spirit of perversion and I found two good ones. I started to repeat them every day. Oh yes, the attacks did intensify, and I almost allowed myself to get frustrated because things seemed to be getting worse than better. However, by now I had learned that the enemy always try to derail me and that this was bigger than just me; I had to push through. I was so close I could taste the freedom.

Chapter 10
Journey To Breaking Free

*A*fter a while, things started to calm down. The more I persisted in prayer, the fewer attacks came my way. The urge to masturbate became less intense and less frequent. Freedom was indeed imminent, and I was rejoicing in the Lord. I longed for a normal life and I felt it coming.

Certainly, I was not out of the woods yet. The enemy resumed attacking me in my dreams but in more subtle ways. There was no nightmare, but I was engaging in sexual activities in my dreams. At first, I did not think much of the dreams because I thought they were only dreams. But as I started to learn more, I learned that my spirit was very much active and whatever happens in a dream defiles the spirit. I learned that you can enter into spiritual covenants with demons by the activities in your dreams. I received this knowledge from Minister Kevin L.A. Ewing through his blogs and YouTube videos. Even though I had stopped entertaining the sex demon physically, I was doing it spiritually (in my dreams) without even knowing. Of course, my lack of knowledge did not exempt me from the repercussion of such actions. Hence the Bible says: "My people are destroyed for a lack of knowledge…" (Hosea 4:6). I learned that things manifested in the spiritual before it happened in the physical. So, I was unknowingly entertaining this spirit in my dreams and not only him, but others too. Eventually, if I had not intercepted, the sexual activities in my dreams would have become a physical reality. The Bible reminds us to be sober and vigilant because the enemy is seeking for the perfect opportunity to devour us.

As time progressed, I seemed to have everything under control. I thought I had overcome the sin of masturbation completely, so I let my guard down. One night, a thought came to me and I entertained it. The memories of all the pleasures I enjoyed in the past were replaying in my mind and I never rebuked the thoughts. The enemy eventually said,

"Why not give it a try? Just once, it's not like you're going to do it every day. It won't hurt; besides, no one would know." I almost convinced myself that he was right, but then I remembered the struggles that I faced to get to the point where I was, and I decided to fight with all I had in me.

I barely survived the night. The following morning, I prayed frantically, "Lord, please help me. I do not want to do this." What I heard next shocked me. The Lord said, "You're lying. You do want to do it. Be honest with me." It was true, I did want to do it, badly. I pulled myself together quickly and went back before the Lord. "Lord, I really really really want to do this, but I know it is not right and I want to please You. I need Your help," I prayed. Then I thought to myself, "if I am going to be totally honest with the Lord, why not just openly tell Him all my desires?" As a result, I spent that entire morning writing to the Lord in very vivid details all the wild and crazy desires that I had bottled up inside me. I emptied it all out to the Lord in prayer and when I was done, I said, "Lord, here they are, take them from me because I do not want them anymore." Then I destroyed the document as a symbol that I was truly done with them.

I felt a heavy burden lift off me and the urges subsided. That was a feeling I needed to embrace because it was the feeling I desired so badly over the years. Freedom! It was finally here. I was overwhelmed with joy, bursting with gratefulness.

Naturally, the enemy did not give up so easily. That same night I went to my bed and had another one of those dreams that was so real I woke up traumatized. One of the desires I had expressed to the Lord in the morning was my desire to engage in sexual activities with a female. Sure enough, the enemy determined that he was going to be my genie and allow me to experience that in my dreams. In the dream, I was lying on my back in my bed and a woman came into my room. Her intention was to act out everything I had written in the morning to God. Thankfully, I was spiritually alert in my dream, so I knew what was happening and I started to resist her. She tried to drug me so she could have her way with me. She soaked a piece of cloth in ammonia and covered my nose with it hoping I would pass out, but I did not. When she realised I was overpowering her, she started to pour the ammonia on me releasing fumes in the air that would no doubt cause me to pass out. I screamed frantically for help as my mother was in the kitchen and my brother was in the room next to me. No one could hear me. I was fighting but I was getting weaker from the fumes all around me. As I was about to pass out, my mom came bursting through the doors and came to my rescue. I woke up with the confirmation that I truly did overcome the spirit of perversion.

The urges continued after that day, but I felt empowered to overcome. I could just shrug it off like it was nothing. I was fully delivered. I could hear the word sex, look in the mirror, take long showers and nothing happened. Wow, this is what true freedom feels like! Thank you, Jesus! I am free! When the enemy comes knocking, I just rebuke him because I am not interested in giving up this freedom for a moment of pleasure. No way!

I later learned that the strongman that controls the spirits of pornography, masturbation and all sexual sins is the spirit of perversion. I attacked the strongman without even knowing it and that is the beauty of how the Holy Spirit works when you have a relationship with Him. That is why the attacks got even more intense when I started praying against that demon. Remember, the Bible teaches that we must first bind the strongman.

If you are also struggling with this sin, you now know who the strongman is. If you are bound by other sins, find out who the strongman is that controls the spirit you are struggling with and pray pointedly against him. We do not have to walk in bondage. God has indeed given us the power to tread on serpents and scorpions; He has given us power over all the enemy's powers (See Luke 10:19). Let us walk in that liberty wherewith Christ has made us free (See Galatians 5:1).

Chapter 11
Have I Settled?

———

One other major struggle for me was the struggle with my identity. My struggle with masturbation only confounded my identity issues. For me, settling means accepting to live below my own standards and the standards that God has set for me. So, to answer the question, yes, I believed I settled.

The trend of settling started when I was eleven years old, after my mother left. I quickly learned to accept whatever came my way as I did not think I was worth much of anything to anyone. Deep down I did not believe that I deserved anything good. A life lesson that I learned early was "the lower your expectations, the less likely it is for you to be disappointed." I never forgot this as the years went by.

There were days I tried to convince myself that there were great things in store for me. After all, that is what my teachers used to say. I always had a desire for success, but it was often overpowered by the reality of what was going on in my life. Still, I knew one day things would be better.

The main area I believe I settled in involves my walk with the Lord. My Christian walk grew to a daily routine of going to church, being involved in church activities and being concerned more about what people thought of me than what God thought of me. You see, finding who you are in Christ is somewhat challenging but even more challenging is maintaining your individuality in the body of Christ.

When I decided to give my life to the Lord, I knew that many of my attributes and practices needed to go; one of them being conceitedness. I always needed to have the spotlight wherever I went. My whole presence was one that dominated the environment. That was very concerning for me as a new convert because I knew the Lord shares His glory with no one. I could not afford for the spotlight to be on me anymore. I simply could not let pride overtake me. I fell into what I

80

call false humility. This mindset led me to decline many opportunities to do things that would display my gifts and talents. Even when I knew I could do well at it and even when I felt the Holy Spirit nudging me to do it.

Moreover, I had a way of dismissing people. Though I was sociable, I believed that most people's opinion did not matter, even persons in leadership. I was so overly confident or arrogant, your opinion of me did not matter. Even if you thought the worst of me, it was not worth my while to try to correct your perception.

When I got saved, however, I believed that as a child of God people's perception was important because I am His ambassador. As such, I went overboard for persons to see me in the best light. I tried my best not to overreact, voice my opinions or do anything at all that would interfere with people's perception of God. At first glance it seemed like a great mindset to have but gradually I started to lose myself. I was no longer outspoken, I no longer pursued justice, I no longer stood up for myself. I became a person who I did not even recognize. People's opinion of me started to rule every area of my life. Some of those persons did not know how influential they were to me. I thought I was doing it to please God and that I was being molded into who He wanted me to be.

I should have realised something was wrong when I became shy. I was never shy. I always pursued whatever I wanted, even if I sometimes made a fool of myself. However, in this new environment, I needed to walk a certain way, look a certain way and talk a certain way. I needed to shed everything that did not align with this new set of standards, so I did just that. I had successfully assimilated into what I call a **box** of people's expectations. This continued for years to the point where I perfectly lost my identity or should I say individuality. While it was a struggle for me to let go of worldly things, it became a bigger struggle for me to hold on to what made Shaniece, Shaniece.

It is not easy to stand out. If you have been in church for any length of time you will know exactly what I am talking about. If you do not fit into that "box", the attacks and condemnation will begin, and they can be brutal.

Many are cultured to fit into two categories which I call the glory positions in churches. You are either a member of the choir/praise team or you are a preacher, otherwise you are just a regular member. If you are not in either of the two categories, you feel left out and start to wonder what role you play in the body of Christ. After a while we become restless and feel like there is no growth, so we settle into the routine of going to church, singing, clapping, socializing and then going home. For me, it was going to church, ministering on the choir, socializing and then going home. I knew there had to be more, but I lost the desire to pursue because of fear of criticism.

Many of us have given up on truly being who God wants us to be and have settled with going through the motions. There comes a time, my friend, when God will call us out of that state and require more of us. That is exactly what He did to me.

Chapter 12
Surrendered

*A*fter many years of settling, it became a way of life. However, there was a feeling of frustration, unfulfillment and restlessness that came over me from time to time. As my personal relationship with God began to grow, my "box" got smaller and more uncomfortable. I was suffocating and dying slowly. Eventually, I lost the drive and motivation to go to church and do church-related activities. I did not understand what was happening to me. Despite the struggles, I pushed through those feelings as though everything was normal. I struggled to stay motivated so just imagine the youths who I was expected to care for. I knew my struggles were affecting them and I needed to pull myself together.

My 25th birthday was approaching, and I felt so depressed and alone. I could not decide what to do to celebrate my birthday, so, the plan was to stay home, watch movies and sleep. About two weeks leading up to the day, a church sister invited me to a conference that was to be held on the same date as my birthday. To be honest, I was not interested. I was saving some money to treat myself on my birthday and I did not think a conference was a treat. She persisted with her invitation. She tried to convince me that it would be a life-changing conference and she knew that it was exactly what I needed. I rolled my eyes and thought to myself, "What does she know?"

On the night before my birthday, I decided to attend the conference because I did not want to remain in my own depressed company that day. Even though I showed up early because I could not help being early for events, I dragged myself to the conference. I found everything to complain about. Finally, the conference started more than an hour late. I was annoyed and not in the mood to socialize.

The first speaker was very good. Her testimony of all that she went through and how God delivered her and transformed her life caused me to reflect on my own life. It caused me to realise that I was blessed and even though I thought everything was going wrong in my life, I still needed to be grateful. After her session, I was engaged in the conference and was grateful that I went. During the worship, I saw the first speaker walking around the room whispering into people's ears. As she whispered to individuals, I would see tears rolling down their faces. I knew she was prophesying to them. I prayed that she would not come near me because I was not interested in any prophecy.

I eventually got so caught up in the worship that I forgot about the speaker who was walking around and prophesying to people. I remember opening my eyes and being startled at the lady standing in front of me. "Sigh!" When she started to talk, I started to lose my composure. She said to me, "God says He has already forgiven you, so why won't you forgive yourself?" Only God knew the traumatic, emotional events I went through in the weeks leading up to my birthday. Tears welled up in my eyes and started to roll down my cheeks. Of course, I was struggling to forgive myself. After all, the hurt I was feeling resulted from the stupid decisions I made. How could I forgive myself?

She went on to say other things to me that confirmed that surely she was speaking as an oracle of the Lord. The final thing she said was that God said I needed to write that book. At first, I was puzzled trying to figure out the book she was talking about. But I eventually recalled all the conversations I had with myself and others saying that I should write a book about the things I have been through and how I overcame. When she was through talking to me, I was overwhelmed with gratefulness. I thanked God for this woman of God and her obedience to the voice of God that day. I pray that she will continue to impact the lives of many others. It was through the words she gave me that my healing process started.

To my surprise, after the conference, I got even more restless. The once comfortable "box" was now my greatest torment. I could not bear going through the same mundane routines of what my life in church became.

One day, while sitting in church, totally lost in my thoughts and unaware of what was being preached, the Holy Spirit asked me, "Who are you?" At first, I thought it was the most absurd question. In my mind I replied, "What do you mean who am I? I am Shaniece, daughter of the most High God." But that was not what He meant, so He asked it again, "Who are you?" That was when I understood the question. The Lord was calling me out. I came face to face with the reality that I did not know who I was anymore.

I was never a people-pleaser. I was never one to doubt myself so much. I was never one to blend in. I know the Lord had blessed me to lead; it comes naturally, yet I would shy away because of fear of criticism and hurt. This question turned my life upside down and I started my quest to finding myself.

I had so many negative things to say about the people in church, but the truth is, they are just regular people. It was my fault for allowing my own experience with them and the experience of others to cripple me. It was my fault for allowing their opinions of me to matter more than it really should. Many of you reading can attest to this, whether you are a Christian or not. In general, we should not allow the opinions of others to affect our lives in such a way that it cripples our growth. At the end of the day, the opinions that matter most is yours and God's.

From the day of that conference, I knew I needed to write this book, but I was fearful. I thought I would write a book on some lovely topic such as prayer, but as I started to seek the Lord, He told me this book was to be about my struggle with sexual purity. Surely this cannot be God talking; He must be crazy. I did not want to be known as the girl who struggled to remain pure throughout her walk with God. People do not need to know that part of my story. My reputation was important to me; I had a certain appearance to keep up.

Months went by and I shoved the idea of writing this book under the carpet. No one needed to know that I had this particular struggle and that was final. It was not up for debate. I went to another conference in October of that year and Crystal Daye was a speaker there. I was following her on social media from the last conference I attended so when we finally met, she recognized my name. I told her I was supposed to be writing a book and she wrote me an inspiring note that sits proudly on my room door as a constant reminder of her encouragement to write this book. God kept on reminding me of my vow to Him that if He delivered me, I would help to deliver His people. Now that He had delivered me, I was required to keep my word.

The following year, on Ash Wednesday, I sat in a prayer meeting empty and depressed because I knew I was not fulfilling my purpose. I was so overwhelmed with pretending that everything was okay when I knew I was unfulfilled. I went outside and started to journal, which was the only way I was able to clear my head. The Lord was flooding my mind with ideas of things I needed to do, and I wrote them quickly. Fear gripped me again and I started to wonder if it was self, or maybe pride was trying to surface. So, I wrote, "Lord, please send me some confirmations." I closed the book and went back into church.

Within a few minutes of sitting in church, I saw my church sister heavily under the influence of the Holy Spirit and I started to pray for her. Then, she held my hands and said, "God said to do what

He told you to do." I was shocked. "I must be hearing things," I thought to myself. She repeated, "God says do what I told you to do." I broke down in tears because it was surreal. I literally just asked the Lord for confirmation and here is this sister telling me these words. She then embraced me and said God told her to do that because I will need courage for the journey.

If that was not enough, while sharing His words of encouragement, my Pastor said these words, "The longer you take to do what you should do, is the more souls that are perishing." I felt like he was staring right into my eyes as he said those words. I knew that was the final confirmation I needed. No more beating around the bushes; no more delays. In that moment I decided in my mind that I was done being fearful. I knew people were struggling with sexual sins and not everyone was brave enough to talk to people about it. I knew people were struggling with finding their identity. I knew I needed to write this book.

Have you ever had an experience where you are all psyched up and ready to do something, but then reality hits you and you start to shy away? Well, that is exactly what happened to me. I knew if I reached out to Crystal there was no turning back, so I delayed yet again. It must have been the mighty hand of God because that very week Crystal reached out to me and she became my coach. Thank God for her, she does not take no for an answer and I can give her no excuses. Gradually, things started to fall into place and my life started to regain meaning. I was now being aligned with my purpose and the restlessness was slowly receding. I made the decision to surrender my life to God, for real this time, fears and all. I realise that this is a commitment I must renew daily.

CHAPTER 13
WALKING IN PURITY

I am so honoured that you have read my book to this point and so I gladly take this opportunity to encourage you to walk in sexual purity. The truth is, we serve a holy God and He requires holiness from us. You do not need to continue to walk in condemnation for that is not the will of God for your life. His Word says whom the Son has set free is free indeed and today the freedom of God is knocking on your door. Unlike mine, the journey to your breakthrough does not have to be so long and hard. I know for a fact that no case is too hopeless for God and if He delivered me, He will also deliver you. I have this confidence because God is not a respecter of persons and what He did for me, He will gladly do for you, if you let Him.

My first advice to breaking free is to **acknowledge** that you have a problem. This is the first step to getting over any addiction, even if your struggle is not masturbation. Until you identify it for what it is, there is no getting over it. For some of you it may be a onetime occurrence that you can easily break away from. That is great, and I want you to pray for others that they may get to the place to do the same. The rest of you may be struggling to break free because somewhere in your mind you do not think you have a problem. You may be viewing it as a haphazard habit that you can easily break away from or maybe it happens so infrequently, you do not think anything is wrong with it. Or maybe you are bound, desiring to stop but just cannot seem to find the willpower to break free. I want you to be honest and acknowledge where you are and start there.

Secondly, I want you to **recognize** that it is a sinful act. You see, the worst thing you can do is minimize the implications of such a practice. Many out there would argue the fact that masturbation is not a sin and it is just releasing sexual tension that has been naturally built up in the body. Do not be surprised if you hear this from even pastors. The main argument is that it is not mentioned by name in the Bible. Whether or not we try to argue it away, it does fall under the category of sexual immorality. My question is, if you are so convinced that nothing is wrong with this practice, then why are you so guilty each time you do it? Why are you so embarrassed by it? Sex is a beautiful act that God intended for two people within the confines of marriage. He never meant for you to have sex with yourself. Think about it; each time you decide to do this act, you are subjecting the Holy Spirit to endure it with you because He dwells in you. If we are to look deeper into this matter, we know that sex is more than physical connection, it is also a spiritual one. You have probably heard the term "soul ties" before. If not, I encourage you to do some research.

Since sex is a spiritual act, when you masturbate, who is your spirit and soul being connected to? Earlier, I mentioned incubus and succubus. These demons prey on people who indulge in these kinds of activities. They are the ones you connect yourself to each time. It starts off very innocent but the more you continue to feed on the desires, the more you realise that your will to stop weakens. The once minor act starts to consume you and your relationship with God will begin to suffer to the point of lethargy and, worst-case scenario, backsliding. There are so many other habits that can stem from this act, such as indulging in pornography, fornication, adultery and many other perverted acts. This is the case because demons operate in gangs and once you open the door for one, it is only a matter of time before the others enter.

Do not be condemned; that is not the purpose of my writing. However, it is important for you to understand what you are dealing with. We do not wrestle against flesh and blood, so we must be aware of the devices of the enemy. God never intended for you to be ruled by the flesh and the enemy can only have the amount of power over you that you give to him. That is why my third advice is to **resolve** in your heart and mind to stop. This step is an ongoing process, but it is very essential you start here and now. Nothing in heaven and on earth can defy your will. God will not do it and the devil cannot do it. Once you decide it in your mind then you are ready for deliverance. I want you to really weigh in the balance all there is to gain by this act (a few minutes of pleasure) and all there is to lose. Write them down, if you need to, but do not skip this step. Next, I want you to assess which is more important to you? How much do you want to grow in God? How much does your relationship with Him mean to you? Once you have made this assessment, and decide it is time for a change, you are ready for step four.

Repent, pray and fast. You cannot fight this battle in your own strength. God has already equipped you with all you need to overcome (See Luke 10:19). Take some time to seek God in prayer and fasting. Now, I am no expert on fasting, and when I was going through the process I did not fast directly about the issue. I know it is a powerful weapon, but I feared doing what many others around me did and starve myself for something that I was not even sure I was ready to give up. Whenever I felt led to fast, I always did it asking God to strip me of everything and bring me closer to Him. The closer you get to God, the more all the bad habits will fall off. I was feeding and strengthening my spirit without even realizing that it was what was needed. And that is what you need to do.

You need to work on building your spirit man. It will be challenging because the enemy will not allow you to just walk out of his camp, but once your mind is made up, then you can do it. Remember, there is no condemnation to them who are in Christ Jesus who walk after the spirit and not after the flesh (See Romans 8:1). In seeking God in prayer and fasting, you are walking after the spirit. That is how you will find strength to overcome this temptation.

Another thing I encourage you to do is to be honest with God. He knows you better than you can know yourself. He knows what is in the deep recesses of your heart; there is nothing you can hide from Him. Let Him know the desires you have and then give them to Him. Let Him know that your desire to please Him is what you are choosing to act upon. If you do not feel this way yet, keep working at it. The more you grow in love with God, the more you will grow in your desire to please Him.

The next thing you should do, and it is probably going to be the hardest of them all, is **talk to someone**. Accountability is an invaluable tool that will help you during this season. The embarrassment of having to tell someone that you messed up can help to keep you clean. It is of paramount importance, however, that you choose someone who you respect, who is confidential and preferably someone more mature spiritually. This walk of faith is not meant to be a lonely one. People are placed around you to help build you up because we all have the same goal and that is to spend eternity with God. If you are struggling with trust issues, ask the Lord to lead you to the right person and I am confident He will.

Finally, **walk in purity!** Let me put you on your guard; it will not be smooth sailing. The enemy knows your weakness and he will come even harder than before. But be aware that this is only his way to weary you and to cause you to doubt what God is doing in you. Do not be moved; keep pressing. Once you have tasted freedom, once you have felt the wholesome beauty of God's presence, then you will not want to lose it. Also, do not beat yourself up if you falter along the way. It happens. A righteous man will fall seven times, but he gets back up and keeps on walking. Never lose your will to break free! Take some time and think about other things you can do to remain pure, then do them. Be sober and vigilant, always keep your guard up. I am cheering you on!

CHAPTER 14

I AM COMING OUT OF THE BOX

◆━━◆◯◆━━◆

I have come to realise that boxing myself into the norms of my surrounding is not only unfair to me but to those around me. After living a substandard life for so long, I finally decided that enough was enough. When God created us, He created us to be individuals. Each of us have something unique that can never be found in anyone else. This means that we all have an impact that we were created to make on the world. Yes, ultimately, we are called to share the gospel of Christ with those we encounter but we can do it in our unique way. There was never another "you" created and there will never be another. Who has God called you to be? As I write, it is speaking to me also because God asked me this question.

Coming Out Of The Box

Today, I choose to come out of the box I created for myself. The box of fitting in and losing my individuality; the box of settling for less than I know I am worth; the box of performing below my abilities and giftings. Today, I choose to be Shaniece, not the one who does what others expect but the one who does what I know God is expecting of me. I choose to listen to the voices and opinions that really matter.

The reality is that everyone will have something to say about you and not all those opinions will be good. At the end of the day, if it does not align with the vision God has placed on your heart, then let it go. You will have to give an account to God on that day as to why you did not fulfill purpose and there will be no one to blame but yourself. The next truth to bear in mind is that the folks who really care about you are the ones who will push you to soar and be all that God created you to be. Those are the voices that matter.

Today, I choose to remain humble; true humility. I choose to walk in my calling and follow God wherever He will lead me. I will not back down, even when it gets challenging. I will hold on to

His unchanging hand. I have been reminded so many times that it is not about me, but it is all about God. Today, I choose to make my life all about God and the furtherance of His Kingdom.

Today, I choose to walk in purity. God chose to dwell in my body, and I will make it a pleasant home for Him. I have tasted freedom and I will not let go of it no matter what.

My prayer for you, my dear friend, is that you too will make a commitment to find who you truly are in Christ and be that individual. It is okay to shine the light that God has given you. He intended for you to shine everywhere you go. Always strive to be holy, regardless of the sins you struggle with. Do not try to make excuses because God does understand. He knows He has given you the tools to overcome, even though you choose to remain in bondage. I echo the voice of the Holy Spirit today and I am calling you out to make a decision in your life. Who will you choose to be? Whose voice will you listen to? Who are you submitting yourself to?

ABOUT THE AUTHOR

Shaniece Wauchope is a Speaker, Author and a certified Christian Life Coach who specializes in wellness. She holds a BSc. in Biochemistry and is currently pursuing her Ph.D. in the same field.

She has always been conscious of her health and sought to maintain a healthy weight and body. This health-consciousness led her to become a weight loss consultant and entrepreneur who retails health and wellness products. Her PhD research sparked an even greater interest in human health when she learned that many of the chronic diseases including 30-50% of cancers can be prevented through lifestyle changes. It is this revelation and her conviction that our body is the temple of God that led her to become a Christian Wellness Coach.

Shaniece is truly passionate about the Lord and, as an active leader in her church, she understands that in the pursuit of spiritual health, it can seem less important to focus on other aspects of health and wellness. In her efforts to fulfill her many obligations to church, home, business and school she often experienced frustration, chronic fatigue and being overwhelmed.

In His faithfulness, the Lord led her on a journey to address, improve and maintain a healthy mind, body and spirit. She then realized that she cannot keep this wealth of knowledge to herself. The Lord has indeed given us everything we need to honour Him in our bodies, and with guidance this objective can be met.

Driven by her passion to help others, Shaniece has made it her mandate to help her fellow church leaders who are invested in multiple activities, be it church, career, family or education to make the mindset shift necessary to transform their health and live a lifestyle of worship through wellness.

To hire Shaniece as your coach or to book her for speaking engagements and interviews, email her at winwithshaniece@gmail.com

www.ingramcontent.com/pod-product-compliance
Lightning Source LLC
La Vergne TN
LVHW051808080426
835513LV00017B/1862